The Sacred Role
of
Intentional Living Feng Shui

9 Accomplishments to Promote
Personal and Planetary Peace

Peace in =

Peace out

♡ Gabrielle

Gabrielle Alizay

Cover Art and Design by Keavon Chambers:
www.keavon.com

Production/Distribution by Ian Gudger:
www.ians.it   (831) 515-TECH

Author Photo by Patricia Mitchell:
patriciamitchellphotography.com

The Sacred Role of Intentional Living Feng Shui

Copyright © 2011 Gabrielle Alizay

ISBN-10: 0-98383968-9

ISBN-13: 978-0-9838396-8-2

Published by Evolution Now ♦ Santa Cruz California

Other Books By Gabrielle Alizay:

Feng Shui For The Rest Of US
What You Can Do Right Now To Change Your Life

The Evolution Solution
Intentional Candle Ceremony's Pathway to Peace

The Daily Support Manual
for
Thriving Conscious Evolution

100th Monkey Theory: A scientific observation, lasting over 30 years, which started in 1952 on the island of Koshima, Japan, with the monkey population. The study began with one monkey learning a progressed behavior. The trend eventually spread, first by word-of-mouth and then, para-psychologically, monkey populations everywhere knew across the oceans and lands, regardless of communication issues. It has been thus applied to the human social condition. When a critical mass number of people achieve knowledge, practice an evolved behavior, adopt a new way of thinking, this new consciousness may be communicated from mind to mind spontaneously spread to the rest of humanity. Although the exact number may vary, this phenomenon reflects that when only a limited number of people know of a new way, it may remain within the group but there is a tipping point at which if only one more person adopts this mindfulness, all of humankind adopts this Evolution.

CONTENTS

"The majority of us lead quiet, unheralded lives as we pass through this world. There will most likely be no ticker-tape parades for us, no monuments created in our honor. But that does not lessen our possible impact, for there are scores of people waiting for someone just like us to come along; people who will appreciate our compassion, our unique talents. Someone who will live a happier life merely because we took the time to share what we had to give. Too often we underestimate the power of a touch, a smile, a kind word, a listening ear, an honest compliment, or the smallest act of caring, all of which have a potential to turn a life around. It's overwhelming to consider the continuous opportunities there are to make our love felt."

Leo Buscaglia, Author and Motivational Speaker

THE FIRST ACCOMPLISHMENT: INVOKE THE CHI

The Intentional Living Role of Chi

"The pacifist's task today is to find a method of helping and healing which provides a revolutionary constructive substitute for war."

Vera Brittain, Pacifist and Author
of *Testament of Youth*

Chi contributes positively to every aspect of life. Thus having good chi flow is one of the most important first steps in home, office, and life improvement. Chi is an invisible, powerful life-force. Another way to understand it: chi is blessing, luck, miracles, joy, health, attention, amplification and interest.

Good chi flow in your home and office means a better life in general. Remember this truth: Your microcosm environment, your home and office, reflects and affects your macrocosm environment, your life at large. Having the influence of chi is a simple, first step to solving problems and manifesting many desires. In order for Intentional Living Feng Shui to bless your home, office, and world in general, chi must be able to find your space.

Sometimes your life can transform just by the establishment of this life-force in your home and office. It is an impressive and necessary initial step in Intentional Living Feng Shui treatments. Do not underestimate this simple, subtle, yet immensely influential deed.

The introduction of chi is oftentimes the missing ingredient which can instantly solve a life issue. Wherever you have a problem, decide where it lives symbolically in your dwelling and determine if chi flow is there. Again, in order for chi to bless the rest of your home, office, and life—it must find your dwelling first.

It is easy to encourage chi to find your home, office and life. Chi is like an honored guest. Treat it as such. Imagine it to be the Queen or King of a country (or the Dali Lama, or a rock star, and so on—whoever *you* deem important) who visits your space for a lifetime of cups of tea.

Action Plan:

- Be certain there is a pathway to the architect's intended front door. A sidewalk or even a make-shift path of rocks leading to the door is equally effective.

- If you have a porch, make sure it is clean of debris and the "catch-all" of life—shoes, baseball bats, kitty toys, potting soil, and so on go elsewhere—not in sight of the path.

- Create a special feel outside the entrance of your home and office (the architect's intended front door). A mat with the words Welcome!, potted plants, a wind chime, and a couple of chairs are all good suggestions on how to manifest an attractive place which "calls" the honored guest, chi, to your dwelling to bless your life. Whatever your individual situation is, use your creativity to craft a distinctive flair. Work this same magic in the inside entrance of your dwelling. The more special, the more sacred—the more blessings bestowed upon you.

- Always remember that as you pay tribute to chi, you honor yourself. When you make anything more appealing for this outside life-force, you can expect positive, sometimes radical improvements to also occur in your life as well.

Carry out this simple Intentional Living Feng Shui Cure **daily.** This will assist in teaching a hugely essential step both for the individual along with amazing global benefits that can occur when each person privately embraces this custom. The world cannot help but shift for the better. This one Intentional Living Feng Shui cure teaches **the art of receiving and allowing**.

Keep in mind that to enjoy and benefit from chi is your Divine birth right and brings with it a host of other magnificent things, including miracles, opportunities, healing, manifestation, abundance, joy, ease and much more. A daily practice of the following cure helps (me) and anyone to learn to accept easiness, flow, and wonder into the day to day.

Try it yourself. Watch the increase of effortless gifts! Keep in mind that the Mouth of Chi is one of the three most important symbols in the entire dwelling. So your front door lets in all the chi of life-force plus a great deal additionally—even if you regularly enter your dwelling through a side or garage door. Because chi is invited and welcomed through your architect's intended front door, the remarkable benefits that can occur with home and office Intentional Living Feng Shui happen because chi is present at the structure and comes willingly anytime it is asked. Results in the microcosm environment translate to magnificent consequences in the macrocosm of the planet. Undeniably.

The World Peace Intentional Cure

1. **The Action You Take:** On the wall to the right, left, or on the architect's intended front door, attach the address of your home (for example—944). If numbers are not in your style or are impossible to affix, a figurine, symbol, or plaque attached to the front door or to the walls on either side of the door will do. These numbers or whatever it is you choose to place to the right, left, or on the front door, is the **Caller of Chi.** To carry out the daily practice (after the initial address numbers or plaque or whatever is placed on or near the front door), it is suggested that you stand in front of your front door—whether it is open or closed makes no difference—and face towards the walkway and street.

Attach the Caller of Chi to the right, left, or on the front door. From then on, optimally every day, summon the chi by facing out from the front door.

If you have forgotten to do your daily summons by standing in front of your front door, it is just as acceptable to do your Intentional Practice remotely whenever you do remember it—from the freeway on the way to an appointment, from your bed where you have spent the last two days getting over a cold, from the movie theatre, as you eat popcorn and wait for the main feature—imagine that you are standing in front of your entrance door, facing the walkway and street.

2. **Visualize or Imagine:** Picture a glitter-like substance which stands for chi (or "see" whatever is in your style) coming down both sides of the road in front of your dwelling. Observe it turning up your walkway and moving smoothly towards the address numbers or your designated object near or on the front door, until it reaches it. Do not be conservative on the amount of chi you see at your door. Exaggeration is good. This is chi—the honored guest. Make the amount of chi large and exuberant.

Imagine chi coming towards you from the street and walkway then surrounding you in blissful support as it enters your home and office.

3. Speak out loud the following Affirmation:

"Now chi easily and effortlessly finds my home (office) and life. Miracles, opportunities, abundance, joy, health, love, incredible financial abundance, incredible Life Path success, Incredible Highest Good Invisible and Visible Helpful People (plus any daily specifics you may require like...the Highest Good Tenant...the Highest Good Publisher for my manuscript....the easeful and healing resolve with (blank)...anything you need) now occurs in every way. Miracles happen every day. This or something better for the Highest Good now occurs."

It is with the regular use of this cure that you can experiment with the before and after of any Intentional Living Feng Shui cure that you shall learn for your Intentional Life. Chi increases the optimistic results of all shifts you make. In order for your results—micro as well as macro—to be impressive, chi must actually find your dwelling. By virtue of the fact that everything you do intentionally in your small world affects your large world, bringing chi to your dwelling on a regular basis has a philosophical effect wide-ranging on the global subconscious mind: struggle becomes unnecessary.

Of course, this idea must be intentionally exercised through the dedicated use of this cure on a daily basis. Life ease is rarely instantaneous. But just as the regular use of affirmations reassigns the grooves of your brain, effortlessness can be programmed and practiced on a daily basis and such perseverance will, without doubt, confidently affect your relationship to life in general.

THE SECOND ACCOMPLISHMENT: PROTECT AND HOLD THE CHI

Add the Protection/Dreams Projecting Factor

"You must not for one instant give up the effort of building new lives for yourselves. Creativity means to push open the heavy, groaning doorway to Life. This is not an easy struggle. Indeed, it may be the most difficult task in the world, for opening the door to your own life is, in the end, more difficult than opening the doors to the Universe."

Daisaku Ikeda, President of
Soka Gakkai International (SGI),
a world-wide Buddhist organization

Without doubt, anytime negativity is removed from a situation—whether it is personal, environmental, or social—it becomes much easier to create your positive visions. The following Accomplishment Parts work in tandem with each other to eliminate various kinds of skepticism from your microcosm home and office so that the macrocosm general world is likewise as clear. Life-dreams as well as ambitious successes are then more assured.

Part A:

The Bagua mirror protects the dwelling that it is programmed to guard.

A Bagua mirror is an octagonal shape, like the outline of an American stop sign. The Bagua is an ancient Chinese image that symbolically says, "Stop. Look around. Proceed with caution." It is more powerful than a regular mirror when activated with intention. Wherever there are destructive intensities as well as the potential irritation from passing foot and car traffic, the Bagua mirror is a very effective defensive force to have on your side.

Because you do not want your hard Intentional Living Feng Shui work to be influenced by, for instance, a sick neighbor or an angry person driving by in a car, it is recommended to protect your space, home, office, and life with a Bagua Mirror.

A Bagua mirror should only be used on the exterior of a building, primarily above the outside of the Mouth of Chi front door.

The exception to this rule is when your individual apartment or office suite exists in an anonymous, larger building; or when it is impossible to hang a Bagua on a building's outside wall. Then with the reflection facing towards the outside part of the building, use adhesive to attach a Bagua mirror above the <u>inside</u> of the architect's front door. Be sure that the reflection part of the mirror faces in the direction of the outside.

Remember to treat a Bagua mirror like a tiger—beautiful, strong, and influential—nevertheless, you would not want the tiger inside your house.

Because it has such a commanding force, the Bagua mirror is the obvious choice to ward off particularly influential destructive forces. Examples would be a brash, loud, alcoholic neighbor, a cemetery located near your dwelling, or even some tension wires that you feel could affect your family's health. Bagua mirrors can deflect, with intention, any and all exterior forces that seem especially pessimistic to your overall health and well-being.

Action Plan:

- Attain a Bagua mirror. It is not necessary to purchase a traditional Bagua mirror, unless that is your style. A beveled, octagonal mirror works just as effectively when programmed with intention.

- Please refer to **Support Services** at the end of the book for instructions on where to purchase recommended Bagua mirror options in made to order **Power Pack Kits™**.

(a) Intentional Bagua Mirror Activation

1. **The Action You Take:** Attach a Bagua mirror (traditional or non-traditional) to above the outside of the architect's front door. It is attached with Velcro® or double-sided foam either to the doorframe or above it. In cases where attaching a Bagua mirror above the outside of your front door is not feasible, secure the mirror, with the **reflection side facing the wall towards the outside**, above the **inside** area of the front door.

Attach a Bagua Mirror to above the outside of the front door.

2. **Visualize or Imagine:** See all negativity, from the front, sides, and behind the building being deflected away from your dwelling by the power of the Bagua mirror (imagine this like shadows, lightning rods, green sickly colored spirals, whatever people faces that appear in your mind, and so on) coming at the front door, only to be thrown away by the reflection force of the Bagua mirror. Then see the glitter-like substance of chi coming through your door into your front entrance.

Imagine all negativity on all levels being deflected away from the dwelling by the Bagua mirror.

3. Speak out loud the following Affirmation:

"Now, all negativity from every direction and every dimension is being deflected away from my home (office) and my life.
Luck, love, health, and abundance to all who enter.
Miracles happen every day.
This or something better for the Highest Good now occurs."

Part B:

The Mystical Alarm System protects the dwelling from unwanted intrusion.

Homes, offices and businesses in China have significantly less intruder break-ins when the occupants hang a *mystical alarm system* on the inside knob of the Mouth of Chi front door.

Simple and inexpensive to make, a mystical alarm is a red cord with one bell attached to it. You can also fasten three bells, five, seven, or even the Intentional Living Feng Shui power number of nine (9) to the red cord. More bells are not necessarily better and are merely a personal design style. Just make sure that you affix an odd increment of bells to your mystical alarm. The alarm system can hang loosely or tightly around the inside doorknob. The tight style is recommended when you have cats living with you. Cats have a confident belief that you hung the bells as a personal plaything for them. This confusion is avoided when the mystical alarm does not droop down from the doorknob. The bell does not have to ring when the door is opened in order to be effective. It is your intention that gives the Mystical Alarm System its effective power.

Action Plan:

- Obtain or make a Mystical Alarm System. It is fine to use traditional alarm systems, but not necessary. You can also use non-traditional ones. All kinds are effective when programmed with intention. Usually they can be created by using simple, red cord with a single (or in odd increments) jingle bell(s). Please refer to the **Support Services** at the end of the book to get instructions on where to purchase recommended Mystical Alarm System options in made to order **Power Pack Kits™**.

(b) Intentional Mystical Alarm System Activation

1. **The Action You Take:** Hang a Mystical Alarm System (traditional or non-traditional) on the inside knob of the Mouth of Chi front door. When putting a Mystical Alarm System on a sliding glass door, hang it from a suction cup with a hook. Remember that it is unnecessary for the bells to ring when the door opens or shuts.

   Hang a Mystical Alarm System on the inside door knob of the Mouth of Chi front door.

2. **Visualize or Imagine:** See that the presence of the Mystical Alarm System on the door keeps out all intruders, whether this is a thief or someone posing as a friend. Imagine this as a force field that surrounds your dwelling and is as tall as your dwelling is high and also includes a basement if relevant. Picture the big, burly thief—you do not need to see a face—unable to penetrate past the force field of light. Next, envision a person who is smiling (again the face is unimportant), but the smile does not go up to the eyes or down to the heart. Your best interests are not in this person's mind. This person also cannot get past the force field of light.

Imagine an impenetrable force field of light
completely surrounding your dwelling, keeping
out all who should not enter.

3. Speak out loud the following affirmation:

"Now I am safe on every level multidimensionally.
Miracles happen every day.
This or something better
for the Highest Good now occurs."

Part C:

Hold Chi in Your Mouth of Chi.

Holding chi inside your building is one of the most beneficial things that you can do for life improvement. This burst of good intention is strongly suggested to be performed inside the front door (the Mouth of Chi). Remember that chi is life force, blessing, luck, healing, manifestation, interest and joy. After you have invited chi to your dwelling and world in general (and this is a daily recommendation), make sure that it stays there. You do not want it symbolically passing through windows, skylights, open bathroom doors, or even down hallways which lead to a back door directly across from the front entry. Always keep in mind that the presence of chi in every Intentional Living Feng Shui shift you perform amplifies results magnificently, so hold it in!

Securing chi in the Mouth of Chi, with intention, is one of the primary steps to transforming—immediately or eventually—impossible or difficult situations into solutions. In fact, major life changes have occurred for many of my clients just by performing this simple intentional act. An acupuncturist brings the healing force of chi to the exact spot that needs regeneration. Likewise, with you as the alchemist, you intentionally and symbolically hold chi in the Mouth of Chi and because the Mouth of Chi front door is one of the most important places in your dwelling, a rise in the frequency of the entire dwelling is undeniable. Get ready for the wonder! This intentional act shall bring remedial, solution oriented results into your broad-spectrum world.

Holding chi in your home and office should be one of the first steps you take, even if you consider this act an experiment. This intentional feat guarantees an energy shift because holding chi in the dwelling is one of the fastest ways to find enlightenment and to walk your spiritual path. And though the resulting changes might not always be pleasant, transformation happens quickly. It makes all phases toward problem-solving and goal manifestation easier—as well as much faster. Holding in the chi is the "Quantum Healer" to all kinds of issue solutions and life dreams in general life. Chi is that powerful.

It is a part of our culture to struggle to accomplish anything of value. This is the reality of hard work, especially prevalent in our Western World. Yet another way to view this drive is that this is your personal chi showing commitment towards a particular goal. This behavior pattern is an outward directed path. In addition to this outward directive of working so hard, hold the chi symbolically in your dwelling as well. This feat brings you, the empowered co-creator, to the **inner** game of achievement. Watch and see how you no longer push against the river of your general world to get to where you want to go.

Action Plan:

- Obtain or make custom chi-catchers for your home/office/life. An effective chi-catcher can be traditional—9 inches of red cord with a faceted crystal hanging from it; or it can be large, showy and obvious, like a disco ball; or calm down…it can be virtually invisible, like a chi-catcher that is made with a small, clear, glass bead attached to a 1 inch fishing line. Suspended from the ceiling with a non-obtrusive color thumbtack (like a white tack in a white ceiling), this chi-catcher is almost undetectable and extremely in-expensive to create. Any chi-catcher which is in your style is just as effective as any other when activated with intention. Please refer to the **Support Services** at the end of the book to get instructions on where to purchase recommended chi-catcher options in made to order **Power Pack Kits™**.

(c) Intentional Cure for Holding Chi in Mouth of Chi and Every Bagua Life Value as well.

1. **The Action You Take:** Suspend a chi-catcher (one of your style and choice) from the ceiling about a foot in, more or less, from the front door Mouth of Chi (or your individual personal room if you live in a house share where the roommates are not interested in Intentional Living Feng Shui).

   Attach the chi-catcher string, cord, or fishing line to the ceiling about 12 inches (use your intuition on where to exactly hang it within this recommendation) from the inside front door with a thumbtack, nail, or hook. The chi-catcher does not have to be 9 inches long to be effective. Odd increments like 1 inch, 3 inch, 5 inch, or 7 inch are fine and many times necessary when the ceilings are short or the person tall.

   Suspend a chi-catcher from the ceiling roughly 12 inches inside the Mouth of Chi front door.

2. **Visualize and Imagine:** Imagine a glitter-like sub-stance (this is your chi representation) filling the entrance, hallway, and every room of your dwelling, from the floor all the way to the ceiling.

Imagine this glitter completely engulfing the entirety of the space—this can take a while to be exact and detailed about filling every room. Be liberal about the amount of chi you imagine filling the entryway and rooms. Remember chi can bring solutions to problems and miracles to everyday life.

Visualize chi essence completely filling every room in your dwelling.

3. **Speak Out Loud the Following Affirmation:**

**"Now the chi to the Mouth of Chi
as well as the chi to Career/Life Path,
Self-Knowledge/Wisdom, Family/Health,
Wealth/Power, Fame/Reputation,
Love Union/Marriage, Child/Creativity,
Helpful People/Travel as well as
The Center Of The Universe
stays in my home (office) and in my life.
Miracles happen every day.
This or something better
for the Highest Good now occurs."**

THE THIRD ACCOMPLISHMENT: CULTIVATE THE CHI

Keep Your Bathroom Door(s) Closed

"We cannot direct the wind, but we can adjust the sails."

Anonymous

The home and office bathroom(s) indicate an intriguing representation of our subconscious psyche. Keep in mind these essential aspects: Intentional Living Feng Shui is a language of symbols, and in this art—water symbolizes abundance—and while the bathroom is a place of water; it is also a place of drains—thus the *bathroom* with its multiple drains, translates into *abundance going down the drain.*

Here is an Intentional Living Feng Shui saying: *Chi is brought by the wind and held by the water.* If we allow our water, which holds the life force of our miracles, healing, opportunities, abundance, joy, and manifestation, to disappear symbolically down the drains of our dwellings, the bathroom is much more than an obnoxious structural vice that must be cured in order for our lives to be marvelous. It holds the keys to our abundance staying intact.

There is, without doubt, a difference in both the feel of a dwelling as well as the responsiveness of the occupants—when the subconscious messages that ring out within the home and office shift away from specific visuals that represent lack. Believe it or not, an open bathroom door symbolizes: "I do not have enough!"; "I do not deserve abundance in my life!" and "There is simply not enough!"

With the Intentional Living Feng Shui treatment of closing the bathroom door(s), you change the sub-conscious read for yourself and others to plentitude declarations like "I have more than enough!" and "I am abundant!" Though this mind-set change does not happen overnight, the eventual mental alteration is guaranteed and assured. It is likewise crucial in this time and space on the planet earth to be surrounded in abundant thoughts and beliefs. It is in the notions of plenty where the planet's immense need for per-sonal, social and ecological solutions shall be uncov-ered and acted upon—that is where our brilliance waits for us; in a land where ideas fall from the sky in an ever-growing multitude of greatness. Keeping the bathroom door closed is how you begin this journey; you deserve the serenity it creates in your microcosm small world of the home and office as well as the gifts this promises on the grand scale of macrocosmic big world continuation.

A bathroom door that remains closed at all times is the first significant step you can take to improve the results in the rest of the dwelling as well as your life. Among the rather lengthy inventory of qualities that chi prefers, know that chi follows the path of least resistance. A wonderful spiritual practice that we could all benefit from—but not so hot when a bathroom door is left open anywhere in the dwelling! Chi, the sacred elixir, who holds your life force, luck, blessing, opportunities, manifestation, healing, and joy, will easily and effortlessly voyage to the exposed drains of the bathroom's open door and disappear down them—whether this lavatory exists near the Mouth of Chi or down the hall and through, for instance, the guest bedroom.

Chi likes to gush and if you are not careful, your miracles and more will end up unappreciated in the local Municipal Sewer Company instead. If shutting the bathroom door is a real concern because you need the bathroom accessible at all times—for instance, the door is left open because of animal needs, like a litter box, consider a pet door installed in your closed bathroom door or use the Hippie Cure. The Hippie Cure is nice also for those situations when there is a the desire for heat in a cold tiled room, light in a cave-like washroom setting, or the personal "closed door phobia" exists.

To create a Hippie Cure: in your own style, find a piece of fabric that covers the open bathroom door area or even an opening which is larger than a standard door and leads into a bathroom. The fabric should **not** be see-through or have eyelets in it, like lace. It should extend from the **very top** of the inside doorframe to the **floor** of the inside doorframe. With a tension rod mounted inside the door support, fix the material as if it is a curtain. Make sure it opens and closes easily as well as completely hides the view of the bathroom. The door is now soft and allows access—by pets, heat if your material is pliable and illumination if you use a bright colored fabric—into the room. For details and visual clarity, see **page 69** of *Feng Shui For The Rest Of Us.*

Do not let excuses keep you from performing this essential bathroom Intentional Living Feng Shui protocol. In many ways, this imperative step—the shutting off of drain access to chi is vital to the success of your overall Intentional Living Feng Shui dwelling of personal and planetary transformation.

The Chi Cultivation Intentional Cure

1. **The Action You Take:** Shut your bathroom door and get in the habit of keeping it closed. If shutting the actual door is not an option, install a pet door or a Hippie Cure.

Shut the bathroom(s) door.

2. **Visualize or Imagine:** Imagine many big balls of glitter-like substance (chi) reaching the closed door or the Hippie Cure fabric and not being able to pass through the barrier of the door or cloth into the bathroom. See the glitter balls bouncing back to all parts of the dwelling.

Imagine chi essence not being able to pass through the closed bathroom entrance and instead filling up the entire space with its magical force.

3. Speak Out Loud The Following Affirmation:

"Now the chi from every area
in my home (office) and life
stays intact and
cannot get through the door (fabric).
None of my chi abundance goes down the drain.
Miracles happen every day.
This or something better
for the Highest Good now occurs."

THE FOURTH ACCOMPLISHMENT: HONOR YOURSELF AND FAMILY

Choose to Sleep on a Bed Mattress that is Free from Past Grievances, Relationships and Traumas

"Life is not an easy matter...you cannot live through it without falling into frustration and cynicism unless you have before you a great idea which raises you above personal misery, above weakness, above all kinds of perfidy and baseness."

Leon Trotsky—Diary in Exile, Entry for April 3, 1935

The master bed, particularly the **mattress**, is the **Symbol of Love** in Intentional Living Feng Shui. Get to know the Feng Shui language of symbols. This dialect is one of the secrets to accurately diagnosing anything in your home and office. When you understand what the symbols are instinctively saying, then you can knowingly fine-tune the situation through the changing of or the repositioning of these signs, and then with intention, amend the outcome of what you are experiencing in your life. Because of the potency of sacred love in all cultures, the magnitude of the bed as one of the three **most important objects in a dwelling** becomes clear. With this in mind, learn this fact: ***do not sleep on a used mattress.***

Mattresses store the patterns, thought-forms, beliefs, and experiences of its predecessors. Whether it is the history in an unknown thrift store special; or the costly mistakes from a relationship or marriage which ended badly; or even if your mother gave you her great "almost new" mattress when she moved, resist the urge to save a buck. You are choosing a path, however hidden and unconscious, that can have grim results to your personal life.

This caution is not for long-term couples who purchased a mattress together 20 years ago. Breathe. You can keep your lumpy, stained, dips-in-the-middle mattress if you want. A new mattress is recommended only when your heart has been "horse-whipped" by a relationship—whether that liaison lasted five years or five minutes. This self-reflection requires honesty. It is rarely easy to admit to being truly hurt when a connection does not work out. And in this case, it could be a rather expensive assessment, but one that more than makes up for itself in the

"Love Bank Account". Sleeping on a new mattress changes the Symbols of Love.

If you are sleeping on a used mattress, be aware of the following:

- A used mattress is typically the hidden factor between what your conscious goal is ("I want a great new love of my life!") and what you actually manifest in your day-to-day life (another lonely Friday night in front of the TV—eating potato chips dipped in chocolate ice cream).

- A used mattress could be the actual reason behind why when you attracted another mate, over time; this new love interest has exhibited similar patterns and behaviors as the ex. This is especially prevalent when the same mattress is used for successive relationships.

- A used mattress could be the unknown cause for nervous tension and anxiety that exists in your current relationship—regardless whether you live together or do not even sleep together on this used mattress. The fact that it exists in your microcosm is enough to affect your macrocosmic connections.

- A used mattress could be a deterrent to manifesting vitality on the physical, emotional, mental and spiritual planes. Thus, become ruthless about knowing the condition and history of your mattress. Make it a priority to replace a mattress if used. You could be sleeping on patterns of promiscuity, failure, betrayal, illness, death, and even various unknown but rather repulsive configurations that come included in the purchase of the "deal of a century" but are really no deal at all to your wellbeing.

- Do not be concerned to have wild abandon with a used mattress Symbol of Love. Go ahead and remove it from your microcosm world. This act will actually serve the hurting planet. Believe me, when you change the subconscious nervous system DNA messages that you absorb whenever you rest or sleep, you are going to feel and pulse a much different vibe. One that enhances the global environment. Peace *does* start in the bedroom.

The news gets better. You will also *not* have to wear this t-shirt:

I Need A Hug…

Mattress Stores Love Me

Landfills Hate Me!

The Neutralization Dedication

**As I let go and genuinely release
into my true nature,
this self-healing act effortlessly creates
generosity, belief in miracles and true abundance
to all who are in receipt of the(se) item(s).
Miracles happen everyday.
This or something better
for the Highest Good now occurs.**

Say the above devotion right before you are getting rid of the mattress, bag of stuff or anything else. This deed of generosity and sharing can be so intended for all of your emotionally-charged-full-of-yuck used mattresses as well as any other "clutter" items that you need released from your microcosm world. This **Neutralization Dedication** is extremely effective when this one rule is followed:

The item(s) must leave your microcosmic universe. No to sister across town, no to uncle who lives in Spokane, no to best friend who just needs a better orthopedic mattress, and no to your down-the-street neighbor. For this **Neutralization Dedication** to be completely real and genuine, you must practice random acts of kindness to strangers.

Need help with how to do that with your stuff? Go to freecycle.org to learn about a local branch near you, plus if one does not exist in the vicinity, get ideas from them about setting up a place of community sharing and humanity where you do live.

Action Plan:

- Research places (bedding stores, on-line storefronts, and wholesale warehouses) where new mattress can be purchased for discount prices. It is not as expensive as you might think. However, if sleeping on a new mattress is a sizable investment for you because you insist on top quality—know that you are likewise seeking an excellence in your love life and emotional/mental balance as well. You will heart thrive by sleeping on a new mattress that will create fresh fairy tale stories about your sacred relations. Viva La Visa!

New Mattress Intentional Cure

1. **The Action You Take:** Stand before your new mattress, futon, foam (or stand before your older mattress that is not brand new but purchased appropriately).

Stand near the foot of the bed, looking at the mattress.

2. **Visualize/Imagine It Already Occurring.** Picture healthy patterns of self-love as well as the sacred love of another person rising up and out of the bed, then surrounding the mattress in joyous glory (see this as pink heart-shaped bubbles rising up from the inside middle of the mattress and then surrounding the mattress surface, sides, and underneath with these pink, sparkly hearts).

Imagine positive and nurturing chi forces wrapping around your bed, creating blessing and optimistic results.

3. Speak Out Loud the Following Affirmation:

"Now I sleep and rest on healthy, self-loving patterns and stories of sacred love. I am surrounded in positive, trusting, romantic energies of well-being.
I am vitally healthy on all levels.
Miracles happen every day.
This or something better
for the Highest Good now occurs."

THE FIFTH ACCOMPLISHMENT: HONOR YOUR PROSPERITY

Clean Your Stove

"Doing the best at this moment puts you in the best place for the next moment."

Oprah Winfrey, International Benefactor

The **stove** is the **Symbol of Prosperity** as well as one of the **top three highest-ranking** icons in the entire dwelling. While the stove is traditionally not given a superior ranking greater than the front door Mouth of Chi or the bed Symbol of Love, it undeniably gains a striking advantage by profiting from the intentionally treated front door, Mouth of Chi, as well as an intentionally treated bed. The Intentional Living Feng Shui Domino Effect is alive and clear. You cannot improve one area of your dwelling (and life) without absolutely touching another. In this case, openly directed Power Objects—the front door and the bed—target their astonishingly potent concentration of their transformational and results-oriented positivism toward the emblem in the dwelling that represents prosperity: the stove.

Without hesitation, a detailed cleaning of your fully operational stove is the next priceless advance you should take to generate major upgrades in your life and world. A meticulous cleaning does not mean a hurried swish with a damp sponge. It means soaking the burners and the removable control dials in soapy dishwater while you conscientiously remove the cooked on crud that has melted onto the stovetop—the elevated continent-like masses of burnt, hardened goop stuck to the enamel landscape. It means carefully eliminating the dribble from the Ghost of Meals Past that has formed vertical lines of colored culinary splendor down the front of your oven door.

It means opening that oven door and risking the journey inside its defiled walls, cleaning off splatters, old food droppings, and scalded bread crumbs. It means turning the black to grey-blue again (or to whatever color your oven boasted before you began to cook in it). For some people, whose lives are so forlorn and lost, but have the good fortune (cough) to get an Intentional Living Feng Shui consultation, it might even mean to pull the stove appliance away from the wall if possible and to clean out the scary accumulations, alive and not so alive, that exist there.

With this one recommendation, I can oftentimes expect to see loathing in the eyes of the sponge holder and I am assured that a return visit is not in my future. Until the Accomplishment is actually taken. Then my phone rings. Laughter. Glee. Vocal chimes of "how-in-the-world-did-you-know-this-was-exactly-what-I-needed?!?" Easy. I happen to be aware, after years of consultations, that cleaning the stove works miracles. Whenever you need a lift in your life— whether acute or chronic—this treatment works absolute wonders.

Action Plan:

- Obtain in advance what cleaning supplies you need to perform a scrupulous, concentrated effort on your stove. While it is better to have a spotless stove than not, regardless of who does the dirty work, the best results are had when the stove is actually detailed by you and not by a domestic engineer or personal assistant. However, if you are physically challenged and need the physical and/or emotional help:

    1. Be present the entire time the stove is being cleaned;

    2. Be sure to add your meditative visions;

    3. And speak your heart-felt statement as explained in the Intentional Cure that follows.

- While environmentally friendly cleaning supplies are strongly recommended, many times, stores that sell and repair appliances have special equipment and cleaning solutions that can be rented or purchased in order to tackle especially difficult, hard-to-clean stoves. Be careful however, as often their formulas are far from environmentally friendly and thus proper hazardous waste removal etiquette should be followed after the clean-up is completed. On every level, make your actions dignified and constructive for all forms of life. The consequences will be that much more outstanding.

- If you bought or rented a dwelling where the stove is beyond all recognition of its original glory because it has years of cooked on mess, welcome to your inheritance of Prosperity Karma. It then becomes your absolute priority to educate yourself on the various steps to take in order to rectify the situation into a sparkling clean Symbol of Prosperity. Make no excuses— the enhanced quality of your future might be waiting behind a pair of rubber gloves and some hard work.

- Perform the following treatment as often as you deem intuitively necessary, even if your stove is not in need of a major revamping. The intentional symbolic worth of your actions is valuable regardless.

Intentional Meditation Cure While Cleaning The Stove

1. **The Action You Take:** In a comprehensive way, clean your stove and oven—top, front, inside, and out. Be detailed and exact. You perform this ritual in your microcosm environment for wide-ranging self and world improvement.

    Thoroughly Clean Your Stove.

2. **Visualize and Imagine:** Throughout the process, which could easily take an hour or two, as you remove the layers of baked on grease, drips, and crumbs, imagine the elimination of blocks, negativity, clutter (real and situational) from your life. If desired, you can also picture political and societal situations that you want eradicated. During the process, you might actually visualize details that exist in your life as well as on the planet that you wish to release and transform. Alternatively, you could free associate throughout the allotted time. Or do a mixture of focused visualization combined with the mind floating through personal and global images. The power of the meditation comes in the awareness that you are performing an act that will drastically better your life as well as the quality of existence. Avoid second-guessing

your effectiveness. Whatever you do during this step is perfect and meant to be. Proceed to step three, after the end of the determined effort of stove clean up.

Imagine Personal and Planetary Optimistic Transformations while Cleaning.

3. **Speak out Loud The Following Affirmation:**

"Now I enjoy the many abundant gifts that occur in my life and in the world because my Symbol of Prosperity is free to broadcast the messages of financial, wellness, love and peace abundance. My health on every level, including the balance of my ego, my cellular formation of true community as well as my ability to receive everything good increases exponentially. Miracles happen in my life and on the planet every day. This or something better for the Highest Good now occurs."

THE SIXTH ACCOMPLISHMENT: HONOR THE POWER OF YOUR CLARITY

Clear Your Clutter

"Sometimes, what feels like surrender isn't surrender at all. Its about what is going on in our hearts. About seeing clearly the way Life is and accepting it, and being true to it—whatever the pain—because the pain of not being true to it is far, far greater."

Nicholas Evans, *The Horse Whisperer*

Clutter surrounds us and everyone has it—even Feng Shui consultants. Surprisingly, clutter is not what you might think and it is uncomplicated to determine what "real" clutter is. And guess what? Clutter clearing is not a chore. It is actually a sacred practice that guarantees physical, emotional, mental, and spiritual gifts in return for the elimination of what is no longer in your best interest to keep around—

surrounding you, your family, as well as your existence in general.

Clutter clearing is one of the most significant as well as rapid ways to see positive results in your world just from taking intentional action in your home and office. It is a supreme problem-solver. It paves the way gloriously for goals of all kinds to materialize on your life path. Clutter clearing motivates, inspires, and discharges negativity in the dwelling, the body, the mind, and the soul. When there is room (symbolically and physically), there is "space" for the good things, which raise your energy, to show up in your life. Get rid of the clutter—then await the offerings to shower you from every direction. For instance—physically, you might receive a new coat or that call from Mr./Ms. Right asking you on a date; emotionally, a big dose of peace could come into your consciousness; mentally, you stop being so hard on yourself; and spiritually, you find you have a greater faith in your Higher Power.

Thus, clutter clearing is a great application for problem-solving life's big and small challenges. Have a dilemma with anything? Clutter clear! Watch and see your world improve! It is also a fantastic tool in conjunction with talk therapy; clutter clearing promises to move stuck energy on all levels (perfect for the *bored-nothing-ever-works-for-me-this-is-a-crock* person) —even if all you are doing is functioning on the third-dimensional plane. Remove the "muddle" from your environment and see how your issues start to let go!

Clutter clearing can be amazingly effective and may accomplish both problem-solving and goal manifestation without a lot of Intentional Living Feng Shui knowledge under your belt. It is a fantastic way to witness just how influential the microcosm environment of your home and office can positively affect the macrocosm environment of your life in general. As you remove the "stuff" in your atmosphere that no longer supports you, you can then assess the profound, optimistic transformations that occur in your daily life and following the micro-macro law—the world in general!

Clutter in your home and office can:

- Make you tired and lethargic;

- Lower your self-esteem;

- Keep you living in the past;

- Affect your body weight;

- Influence the way people treat you;

- Confuse you;

- Lead to procrastination;

- Cause disharmony;

- Make you feel ashamed;

- Depress you;

- Distract you from essential things;

- Represent turmoil on other levels—emotional, mental, and spiritual.

Clutter in the home and office is often disregarded because:

- The "stuff" around you feels safe;

- You don't want to change comfort zones;

- You use clutter to fill up your home and office to try to slow down the speed of your life (wrong plan—completely ineffective);

- You suffer from poverty-consciousness (which is not just about money)—but the feeling of lack about anything—money, love, health, and so on.

The Clutter Test

The true Intentional Living Feng Shui definition of clutter:

If something (an object, picture, chair, table, memorabilia, person and so on) lowers your energy (because it, for instance, reminds you, consciously or subconsciously, of a lazy ex-partner), the object is clutter. This something should be removed from your environment.

In fact, if the only thing in a room is a table—and that table lowers your energy (it reminds you of when you pay the bills on it and you barely have enough each month to cover your expenses)—then guess what? The table is clutter and by default, so is the room. And the quality of that room affects the quality of your life in general. Regardless if you *think* you cannot afford to replace it. At least remove it from your environment. You will be glad you did. An empty place in the room as well as the blank wall where a picture used to hang is immensely more positive for you than the existence of a cluttered object which reflects to your subconscious that which is compromised from your true visions.

If something *raises* your energy, in other words you absolutely love it (makes you "pop"—

think effervescent), it serves you and your setting. Keep it.

The Bonus Effect of Clutter Clearing: Gifts on the physical, emotional, mental, and spiritual levels come to you when space is made. So clutter clear and get ready for the personal and planetary miracles.

How do you apply this Clutter Test?

- Look at an object—thing, place, or even a person. Feel your energy field. Does this object or person raise or lower it?

- Another way to diagnose or say this: do you love it? Does it make you feel instantly happy?

- Raise or lower? Raise or lower? With something you consciously and subconsciously vibrate with—there are no stories, no care-taking, sentimentality, or mental narratives. It makes you feel happy and at peace. You smile instantly.

Things to remember when diagnosing any item for its potential clutter factor:

1. **The mind does not choose if an object is clutter.** It is determined from the immediate feelings in the heart and gut. The more intelligent you are, the more you may need assistance from a friend or spouse to help you in turning off your "thinker" so that your diagnosis is accurate. The goal is to verify things with your heart and gut.

2. **Your analysis test (*is this 'something' clutter or no? Does it raise or lower my energy?*) with any item is made in less than five seconds.** It is instant—if you take too long determining the status of an item, more than likely it is clutter. Things which are neutral for you (no real raise or lower response) are not good enough— they "read" clutter and you ideally only want that which makes you pop in your environment.

3. Thus, find the **barometer object** in your home and office. This is determined when you look at something, do the clutter test (raise or lower?), and just nod and smile. No stories, no pauses. You know that this item makes you excited in a great way. Then compare this item against anything you feel uncertain or question. It is amazing how the barometer object helps to bring clarity about indecision regarding the clutter status of other things in your environment. With this instant and rapid behavior pattern in mind, using

only your heart and gut, it is simple to clutter clear an entire large room, full of stuff, in less than two hours.

More things to remember when doing a clutter diagnosis:

- **No care-taking** (*but my partner, my child, and so on… gave that to me…*). If it lowers, it is clutter. This does not mean that you treasure your loved ones any less. This is for the benefit of you, which in turn will be an advantage for them.

- **No sentimentality** (*this dried up rose was given to me by my high school sweetheart…*). If it lowers, it is clutter. If it raises, then display it for all to see.

- **No future time traveling** (*I might need this someday, I better keep it…*or even *this might fit me again, if only I lose twenty pounds…*). Clutter clearing is about staying present. Does it raise or lower your energy right now?

- **No apologizing when something raises your energy** (*this is embarrassing, but I love that ratty old chair. It is so comfortable and soft!*). Clutter is subjective. Trash for someone else might be treasure for you. What matters is that your environment works for you and makes you feel good. This is when goals, human actualization, as well as miracles have a clear conduit to create a sacred existence for you.

- **Clutter existing on the physical signifies issues that need attention on the emotional, mental, and spiritual level as well.** Intentional Living Feng Shui is a language of symbols. Feng Shui clutter holds the symbolic meaning that if stuff exists on the physical plane in any room of any one of your Intentional Living Feng Shui Life Value areas—like love, money, health, career, and so on—then it is clear that issues also exist on the emotional, mental, and spiritual plane as well.

Clutter is thus an incredible diagnosis tool. Clear the clutter then watch and see your concerns on these other planes free up as well. The ruthless and dedicated clearing of the clutter in your environment can release stored and long forgotten grief, anger, and fear that has been accumulated in your cells. It can unleash hidden low self-esteem and self-worth locked inside your system and heal them. It can also reveal trust and boundary issues, rage, and the dark side of the human nature that we all try to suppress. Clutter clearing cleanses you on every level. It is that powerful. To completely revel in the purification that is found when clutter clearing is combined with authentic healing, be sure to perform **The Neutralization Dedication**, found on page 34.

Believe it or not, this is a huge gift because the short amount of time that you feel the discomfort of human emotions will pay you back a thousand-fold. You become free. It is a splendid feeling that can lead to Life Mastery. Clutter clearing is the one of the **best** (if you <u>do</u> the clutter test) and **first steps** to significantly purifying any environment of your home, office, and life. It is that impressive.

Along with physical clutter in your home and office—be on the look-out for situational clutter as well. **Situational Clutter** is the presence of stressful actions that need to be taken in order to bring peace and resolve to the emotional, mental, and spiritual part of your person. Examples of situational clutter: the need to make a doctor's appointment, the unwritten letter, the payment of a long-standing bill, the dealing with back taxes or other legal/financial/personal issues and so on. It is still entirely possible to enjoy the many positive gifts of clutter clearing when the "loose ends" are resolved in your life.

Intentional Cure before a Physical Clutter Clear of a Room, Closet, Drawer, and so on and before a Situational Clutter Clear

1. **The Action You Take:** Regard the area in which you intend to perform the Clutter Test or consider the activity that you must perform to eliminate the situational clutter from your life.

   Regard Your Potential Clutter.

2. **Visualize and Imagine:** Picture that you are incredibly courageous and effective in eliminating objects that do not raise your energy. See that the items (or the situations that exist) have a dark sickly energy field on them. See yourself putting them in paper bags and removing them from your space—for instance you walk them to the trunk of your car where you then drive them down to the local thrift shop (or see yourself performing whatever relevant action is necessary to transform the issue—make the phone call, write the letter, pay the bill, make the doctor's appointment, and so on.) Then picture the multileveled gifts that come to you because you have made physical, emotional, and symbolic space in

your life (see this as a shower of glitter-like chi gently and easily falling down from the sky into your outstretched arms. If you have a specific idea of what kind of "gift" you desire: like physically—a new stereo or more money; emotionally—a greater sense of self-love and worth; mentally—more peaceful thoughts; spiritually— an increase in faith, feel free to add those visions to the gently falling glitter that comes to you effortlessly. They float to your waiting open arms, like a cloud).

Imagine that you easily discern the physical clutter or perform the necessary action to clear the situational clutter and that the physical, emotional, mental, and spiritual gifts come to your open arms.

3. **Speak Out Loud the Following Affirmation before you begin the clearing:**

"Now, I easily clutter clear my space multidimensionally—eliminating effortlessly all that does not serve me. Because I create the physical, emotional, mental, spiritual and symbolic space in my life, gifts on every level including (place specific desires here) shower down on me. Miracles happen every day.

**This or something better
for the Highest Good now occurs."**

THE SEVENTH ACCOMPLISHMENT: HONOR YOUR VISIONS

Know and Use the Power Walls and Power Spaces in Your Dwelling to Solve Problems and Manifest Life Dreams

"To confine our attention to terrestrial matters would be to limit the human spirit."

Stephen Hawkins, Theoretical Physicist

It is good to understand the role of *Power Walls* in your dwelling and how when properly developed, these places can have a majorly buoyant influence on your life. A wall becomes a *Power Wall* and a table or floor area becomes a *Power Space* because you see them, consciously or subconsciously, more often. They are often located in places across from everyday activities that require your presence in a certain location on a regular basis. You choose your Power Walls and Power Spaces when you figure out what walls and areas capture your attention, even involuntarily, on a recurring basis.

By deliberately activating pictures and statuary in these areas, you are knowingly amplifying the affirmative effect that imagery has on the creation centers of the being. Use these places to your advantage. Activating the art and symbols in these zones will give you positive life results very quickly.

Examples of Power Walls and Power Spaces:

- **The wall and area you see every time you lay your head on the bed pillow, as well as the wall and space you see, consciously and subconsciously, when you wake up each day.** They can be the same or not.

- **The first wall and space you consciously and subconsciously see when you enter the front door, or even from the garage door to the dwelling before and after a day at work or running errands.** The wall/space is usually across the room from the front entrance and also can be the area of space on the back of a closed door. Wherever it is, it captures your interest, even reflexively, when you enter the dwelling.

- **The wall and area across from your work desk.**

- **The wall and area across from your easy chair, perhaps even above the television.**

- **Any wall or space in your home and office that catches your interest, however fleeting, on a frequent basis.** The imagery on your walls, tables, and floors is inarguably one of the most significant adaptations you can make throughout your entire dwelling. The simple act of deliberately choosing pictures to replace ones that merely hang, or exchanging the statuary so that it reflects what it is you truly desire in life, has the power to transform your world spectacularly.

- Keep in mind that the subconscious mind, the power center for any goal manifestations, sees its commands in images and symbols. While it is very easy to become use to and in fact, not to even consciously notice anymore that which surrounds you in your dwelling, your subconscious mind perceives everything, every time, and everywhere. The subconscious mind never misses a beat and is a superb manifestor of whatever it is told to create. More often than not, what a person consciously claims and what the wall and home/office imagery (the subconscious beliefs) reflect are two disconnected messages. Usually, the wall images as well as the room statuary reveal the "as is" reality of the situation, regardless of the person's desires.

- For example, if a person seeks to ignite her/his love life—typically, the images on the wall presently verify that the person is alone or feeling solitary in a marriage or relationship (a painting of a beautiful woman, sitting by herself near the shore of a large lake, staring off into the horizon—lovely and lonely; or a statue of a man in a yoga position next to a painting on the wall of a majestic lion sunning in a field—two splendid, but solitary beings). The need to replace such works of art is not meant as a judgment of aesthetics, styles, or standards. But the imagery does not support important principles taught in Intentional Living Feng Shui. You want the art in your dwelling to illustrate to you on all levels that your goals are precious, possible, and happening in this moment. Results in your world will then become extraordinary as your dwelling becomes not only your home and perhaps a workplace, but also your manifestation tool for a life well lived.

Thus, apply the "prepare as if" principle to every Power Wall and Power Space in your dwelling. Surround yourself with visual descriptions that indicate your goals are reachable, practical and happening now. With the igniting of your love life example, the images do not have to be only human reflections. A forest of trees, a vase of flowers and even a field of horses are each legitimate to the subconscious mind that seeks association metaphors—whatever is in your style and design—as long as there is the certainty that more than one can and does exist. Such visual messages of alliance go much farther and are exceedingly more effective at manifesting any goals of coupledom than countless lonesome nights perusing the personal ads on the internet dating site. Or at least do both—then watch and see results.

Some samples of replacement imagery.
You desire more:

- **Wealth**—A picture of people dancing, holding baskets full of fruit (harvest is already here)/A scene of Fall/harvest trees.

- **Health**—An exercise or yoga class of athletic people doing some activity and laughing/Horses running at full speed through a field.

- **Love**—A couple slow dancing in the moonlight/Two wolves touching each other on the nose.

- **Joy**—A group of obvious friends, holding hands with each other and smiling/Colorful, vibrantly healthy flowers blooming.

Remove imagery from the walls or off tables and floors that does not serve you. Take your time replacing the imagery. Do not be afraid of the bare wall or empty table. See it as a clean slate, a clear palette, or a blank canvas onto which you will reinstate things consciously to affect the condition of your subconscious mind so that it can perform marvels for you. Know that gifts—on the physical, emotional, mental, and spiritual plane—present themselves when space is made. Release the visual clutter and the offerings shall appear!

Take charge of what you are telling yourself—a simple but potent place to begin is acknowledging what hangs on your walls and exists around your dwelling. Enjoy uncovering the clues to why love, health, and self-balance in your life might be anything less than satisfactory!

Power Image Intentional Activation

1. **The Action You Take:** Hang the picture/photograph on the wall or place the statuary on its appropriate shelf or floor. Be sure that your art honors the theories of what kinds of imagery reflects the ideal in your day-to-day life.

Hang your image. Find a place for your statuary.

2. **Visualize and Imagine:** Observe the picture or statuary and then envision how the image projects to your subconscious mind to create new brain synapses of incredible confidence and knowledge on the intuitive, cellular level. This ultimately manifests whatever it sees metaphorically from the Highest Good place (See this as blue chi light (blue glitter) emulating off the picture (statue) and entering into the top of your head and traveling throughout and down your body. You smile.)

Imagine that the image or statuary showers you with beams of healthy, abundant, brilliant, happy light.

3. Speak Out Loud the Following Affirmation:

"Now I am positively affected
by the imagery that surrounds me.
I easily create my Highest Good
goals and dreams for myself and for the planet.
Miracles happen every day.
This or something better
for the Highest Good now occurs."

THE EIGHTH ACCOMPLISHMENT: HONOR YOUR LEISURE, REST AND COMPLETIONS

Practice The Red Sheet Intentional Cure To Increase and Create Passion Or Improve Health Or Enrich Your Financial Reality

"Nothing happens by itself...it will all come your way, once you understand that you have to make it come your way, by your own exertions."

Ben Stein, Actor and Commentator

Rarely does an Intentional Living Feng Shui Accomplishment get as much positive attention as this one—perhaps because of its remarkable effectiveness and almost instant gratification. I have received a great amount of encouraging feedback from many "satisfied" customers. Here is why:

The Red Sheet Intentional Cure can either:

1. **Increase passion and intimacy in a current relationship,** regardless of the years that the two of you have been together.

2. **Broadcast to the Universal Air Waves a message for the manifestation of your love partner** (if this is what you seek or is in The Highest Good).

3. **Improve your well-being and vitality on every level**—whether you have health challenges on the physical (an illness or chronic pain), emotional (illness or imbalance, the need for a greater sense of self-esteem, self-worth, the healing of grief, anger, and betrayal), mental (a lessening of obsessive thinking and rigid belief systems), spiritual (a yearning for a bigger trust and faith in your Higher Power), or a combination of them all.

4. **Boost your financial climate.** Yes, money.

Such promises are spine tingling and captivating. However, the Red Sheet Intentional Cure is powerful medicine and not to be taken lightly. It is important to the overall success of this treatment to **only** choose one of the above desires and focus the programming of your red sheet on this single request exclusively. Then when this desire manifests or you experience a core readiness to encode something else—update the mission of the red sheet.

For instance, many times a client is desperate for a love mate but it is clear that self-esteem and self-worth are in such a need for healing that to attract a companion with the client's current emotional condition would have disastrous outcomes. Thus, I more often than not suggest the coding first of the client's emotional health to feel deserving of a Highest Good love partner *before* the actual transmission is put out to the Universal Manifestation Map for a true love partner. When the distressing mood is improved, the red sheet can then easily be reprogrammed to call out for the beloved.

The Red Sheet Intentional Cure teaches patience (the *all good things come in time* theory) as well as the preparation to keep "your eyes on the prize." This training is purely subconscious however; once the intention is set—you can consciously relax, sit back, and then marvel at the results. This remedy coaches you that the aims of your dreams are possible and realistic—and anything that is placed with intention and is in alignment with your Highest Good Big Picture Vision—is attainable.

Results from the Red Sheet Intentional Cure can only be assured when proper Intentional Living Feng Shui bed protocol is followed. Ideally, a new mattress purchase should happen before the experimenting with the red sheet treatment begins, especially if such an execution is necessary to your overall love and health well-being. Sometimes however it is not possible to get a new mattress now, so then experiment with the Red Sheet Intentional Cure with your current mattress. But first do the **Used Mattress JuJu Cure** found of **page 73 of** *Feng Shui For The Rest Of Us.* **Do not** use this cure as the replacement to getting a new mattress or to not making such a purchase an absolute priority. And know—when negativity, trauma, and limited beliefs from your Symbol of Love mattress are no longer influencing you, the ability to attract and keep the affirmative, advanced realities becomes much more achievable.

Action Plan:

- Obtain a red sheet that is closer to the color of red than maroon. It is possible to purchase individual sheets in lieu of buying an entire set. Just be certain that your new sheet is as large as your mattress. For instance—a queen-sized mattress requires a queen-sized red sheet—either fitted or flat is acceptable. It is better to purchase a king-sized red sheet than to sew two twin sheets together for the purpose of this Intentional Cure. It is also satisfactory to use a big enough piece of red fabric if you cannot find an appropriate bed sheet.

- Buy a new red sheet or cloth for this Intentional Cure, even if you already have a large enough red sheet in your closet.

- To insure outstanding effects with the Red Sheet Intentional Cure, follow these bed protocols:

  1. The bed should reside in the Empowerment Position (when you lay your head on the pillow, you can see the door to the bedroom without having to turn your head sideways either way).

  2. Purchase a new mattress or sleep on one that was purchased either with a current mate or after a traumatic event like divorce, death, (and so on) has already taken place and the memories do not "live" in the mattress DNA.

  3. Sleep on a mattress that is a double, queen, or even king as a single mattress does not suggest the symbolic message that there is "room" for another—whether that "room" is a person or the emotional space to heal negative love and health patterns (single mattress okay for kids and teenagers).

  4. Keep your mattress off the floor—whether this is on a frame or a make-shift lift is unimportant—chi needs to revolve around the

mattress for best results, even if the elevation is a mere inch.

5. The bed should not have anything stored under it. Keep a pathway for chi free, clear, and unobstructed so that it can revolve around the mattress.

The Red Sheet Intentional Cure

1. **The Action You Take:** Place the red sheet or red cloth between the box springs and the mattress. A fitted sheet is a bit easier to secure over the box springs once the mattress is placed on top of it again, but this is not necessary. Alternatives might be to situate the sheet/cloth between a mattress, futon, or foam and the bed platform if a box spring does not exist. While you may place the red sheet or red cloth under a mattress that rests on the floor—such an option is not recommended, as a bed on the floor does not allow chi to circulate properly around and under the mattress.

Place the proper sized red sheet between the mattress and the box springs or whatever alternative bedding that you have.

2. **Visualize and Imagine:** Picture that every molecule of the red sheet travels up into every molecule of the mattress which travels up into every cell of your body, programming each cell with this reality: (for instance) you and your mate are, like lightning, attracted and excited on all levels with

each other (see this as hearts and firecrackers and smiley faces filling you and your mate's cells and igniting both of your senses...then use your imagination);—or the perfect fantasy love partner—no need to see her/his face—shares your bed and...use your imagination;—or health on the physical, emotional, mental, and spiritual is vital and strong (see this as the red circles that travel into the cells turning into vibrant green light and see yourself smiling, strong and active—on all levels...use your imagination);—or that money comes to you easily and effortlessly (see this as an image of you standing with your arms open while 100 dollar bills fall all around you and money is stuffed and falling out of every pocket as you smile and share your wealth...use your imagination).

Imagine vibrant red energy infiltrating from the red sheet, through the mattress into the subconscious, conscious, physical, emotional, mental, and spiritual cells of your being, bringing peace and fulfillment of your imaginings. You smile.

3. Speak Out Loud This Affirmation:

"Now every molecule of the red sheet (cloth) travels up into every molecule of the mattress which travels into every cell of my body programming it with this reality, I am:

(full of passion and desire for my beloved as my beloved is for me)...

Or: (turning my fantasy into reality as I enjoy my Highest Good Love Partner)...

Or: (healthy and vital...free with well-being...strong in my esteem and worth)...

Or: (flush with money and generous with my outflow because abundance comes to me easily and effortlessly)...

Miracles happen every day.
This or something better
for the Highest Good now occurs."

You only have to program this affirmation ritual once though a reactivation as often as you need or feel so inspired, is strongly recommended. Also, your priorities might change and a new programming is all that is required. Let your intuition guide you.

THE NINTH ACCOMPLISHMENT: CULTIVATE LIFE MASTERY

Conceal Your Television When it is Not in Use

"Be who you are and say what you feel, because those who mind don't matter and those who matter don't mind."

Dr. Seuss, Author and Sage

There exists a central icon in your dwelling that often goes unnoticed because it holds such common placement in the everyday life. However, its questionable impact on the quality and worth of your life is vast. An untreated television—complete with its symbolic translations—can be like having a loaded gun pointed at you in the microcosmic small world of your home and office.

Feng Shui consultants can be very serious. This is good news for all concerned.

While it is undeniable that the television is one of the greatest communication tools ever invented for humankind—having the astounding potential to connect, exchange ideas, as well as convey cultural wisdom and messages—the kinds of "programming" we receive regularly whenever we watch the television or even just listen to the dialogues for company as we do other things around the house—rarely reaches the true promise for networking, healing, and planetary poise. Clearly, there are many educational, positive, and environmental/politically active broadcasts on the air; but in general, the television's images—both visual and auditory—are:

- Violent and fearful.

- Downbeat and cynical, even if funny.

- A worldview that is without hope—the morning, noon, and evening news rarely report anything but tragedies, economic concerns, and the negative shenanigans of unbalanced, unhappy, and unhealthy people.

- A worldview that has only one body image per each gender—female thin and male muscular.

- A worldview where being independently financially wealthy is the norm (*This Soap Opera Life Is Fabulous* Theory).

- A world view where dramatic, scheming, self-serving, superficial behaviors are both applauded and admired as many character's issues are "resolved" within a 30-60 minute episode segment.

- A worldview where "reality" is presented and yet the installments are clearly pre-rehearsed, staged, and unoriginal.

- A worldview where the watching audience holds a star struck attitude about actors—both their ability to imitate as well as the details of their normal everyday lives.

Please know however—it is hardly the point of Intentional Living Feng Shui beliefs to forbid television watching. If that were the sad case, I'd miss out on those sit-coms I'm addicted to as well as that intrigue of finding some dram or com that will make me cry or laugh.

No, the television is still the most entertaining invention since self-massagers. And it is very important that all of us maintain an equilibrium between the seriousness of our lives with the equally important periods where laughter, chimera, leisure, even distractions fill our heads for a soothing vacation into Never-Never Land.

It is when we are relaxed and rested that our unique genius is found.

But here's the thing:

We are not listening enough to our inner voices. Our God-source, our guides, some of our beloveds on the other side, walk with us now, speaking wisdom. We are not hearing though. We must listen in order to gain this insight and understandings. Within all of us sing the keys of solutions for both inner and outer harmony.

This makes the Ninth Accomplishment extremely crucial to integrate in your home and office. Since Intentional Living Feng Shui is a language of symbols, the television, whether on or off, puts out the above-mentioned inventory of confusing, pessimistic symbolic messages towards you at all times—24/7. This makes it very difficult to hear our inner intelligence and grace.

It makes little difference if you couch potato it in front of your favorite shows on a regular basis, hear the morning news from another room, or have the television completely turned off except on Wednesday night, when there is a prime time line up that captures your attention for a three-hour slot of back to back's.

The messages hit your subconscious mind in a subtle or not-so-subtle onslaught of teachings that can easily drum in discouraging images about your-self—affecting your self-esteem, self-worth, self-image, professional merit, relationship satisfaction, sense of planetary dread, and so much more. The true influence of the television does not rely on the power of electricity. Symbolically, it transmits into your individual microcosm environment at all times—whether on or off. It is important to control these waves of communiqué. It is vital to balance the inner message with the outer.

While the networks tell us that it is we who "de-cide" on the ultimate programs that are aired—the level of consciousness, evolvement, and lack of promise of television shows in general—reflect, to a large degree, a pervasive denial, melancholy and complacency. At this rate, we may just watch the end of the world on a two hour documentary special.

In the social, environmental global crisis we are in, this is hardly the symbolic tool to be broadcasting so intensely into our microcosm environment and sub-conscious nervous systems. It is one that indirectly, consciously and subconsciously—asks us to stay asleep—to instead laugh at the antics of the hilarious single mother every Tuesday night, to cry at the dra-matic movie tragedy of the family who must relocate because the father is ill, as well as to capitalize on the ease of changing channels.

If brutal and graphic details of cruelty to humans, children, animals, and the earth do not supply the needed numb out in order to emotionally prepare for work tomorrow, then hit the remote. Ahh, here is a channel where a stand-up comedian shifts minds into the surface merriment of a skit about "nothing."

With all things—especially demonstrated by the symbolic good/bad potential of the television—balance is imperative. It is urgent that equilibrium is struck—for the ultimate restoration of ourselves, our communities, as well as the planet. The Ninth Intentional Living Feng Shui Accomplishment teaches this balance of inner to outer. It calms you, bringing your exchanges with others into a new, kinder place.

In addition, this intentional television cure has more benefits. Couples as well as families have improved every aspect of their interactions and intimacy with each other when the television is no longer the predominant feature in the household. The intentional cure is easy to do and incredibly successful at bringing forth a communion energy of kinship.

You do not have to watch television less. But this Ninth Accomplishment adds consciousness and command to your environment. It allows the potential of the inner voice to join with frequently heard outer voices to likewise contribute to authentic global resolutions.

So pass the chips and please move over. I totally love this show.

Action Plan:

- Choose a piece of fabric in your style—color, texture, and design are unimportant—as long as you love it. This fabric shall cover the television set or at the very least—the television screen. Velcro® can be attached to the top of the set on either side, along with the other part of the Velcro® affixed to the fabric to make a low-maintenance, perfect cloth barrier for the television screen.

- If a cloth is not in your style, it is also perfectly acceptable, although more expensive, to obtain a wooden media center to house your television. When the television is off, the wooden doors remain closed.

- For best results, perform this Intentional Cure whenever you turn off the television. With practice, in a very short time, this television treatment will take only about 20 seconds to carry out but will significantly improve your mental and emotional state of well-being. It is worth the learning curve.

Intentional Cure for Every Television in Your Dwelling

1. **The Action You Take:** After choosing a piece of fabric or a wooden media center, cover up the television screen after you finish watching it each time with the fabric or simply close the wooden media doors (visual diagram examples of this are available in **Feng Shui For The Rest Of US Page 103**).

**Cover your television screen
with a piece of fabric
or shut the media doors
where it resides inside.**

2. **Visualize and Imagine:** Picture the cloth (or the closed wooden doors) creating an impassable barricade that completely block T.V. land's peculiar and fantastical ethics from entering into your room, dwelling, and life. See this as dark clouds, lightning rods, sickly colored curly cues and so on from the T.V. screen unable to pass through the energy field blockade of the cloth or wooden doors. See that any actual and symbolic negative television principles, ideals, and violence being reflected back to the TV screen.

"See" that the cloth (doors) creates an impassable energy field which stops and blocks any

negativity and situational clutter from entering into the subconscious and conscious field of the room.

3. Speak Out Loud This Affirmation:

"Now all negativity, faulty value systems, unrealistic principles, as well as anything that does not assist in the support of high self-love, self-esteem, self-image and self-worth standards,
stay inside the cloth (wooden) barrier and cannot get through to affect my room, home (office) and life.
I take my life seriously and know that my presence is of value and merit to myself and to the world.
Miracles happen every day.
This or something better for the Highest Good now occurs."

RENEWAL

I am all about the new beginning. After all, realistically—what else is there?

And here is the fortuitous thing. Put into action these Intentional Living Feng Shui Accomplishments in your home and office. Teach your family, friends and neighbors.

Your life heals. The world around you heals.

The planet thrives.

Nice.

SUPPORT SERVICES

The Intentional Living Feng Shui
Second Accomplishment

Power Pack Kits™
Mouth of Chi Intentional Cures

Included in the Organza Bag:
Bagua Mirror; Mystical Alarm System; Chi-Catcher;

All of Gabrielle's relevant Intentional Ritual
and Affirmations

The Evolution Solution
Intentional Candle Ceremony's Pathway to Peace PDF

The Daily Support Manual
for
Thriving Conscious Evolution PDF

Feng Shui For The Rest Of Us
What You Can Do Right Now To Change Your Life PDF

Available at
Gabrielle Alizay's content-oriented website with books,
products, services and free subscription to her V-blog,
The G-Buzz:

www.homepeace.com

Evolution Now
Publishing Company

ABOUT THE AUTHOR

Gabrielle Alizay has been an international Feng Shui con-
sultant and teacher for over 25 years, is the author of several
books, as well as being a scientist of the miracle. She man-
ages the-outside-of-the-box web site: www.homepeace.com
which offers viable tools towards Human Consciousness
Evolution, the way to personal and planetary peace. She
lives with her family in Santa Cruz, California.